BRITTANY KAY BAEZ

The Anxious Mama

50 Ways to Find Peace in the Chaos

Copyright © 2022 by Brittany Kay Baez

All rights reserved. No part of this publication may be reproduced, stored or transmitted in any form or by any means, electronic, mechanical, photocopying, recording, scanning, or otherwise without written permission from the publisher. It is illegal to copy this book, post it to a website, or distribute it by any other means without permission.

Brittany Kay Baez asserts the moral right to be identified as the author of this work.

Brittany Kay Baez has no responsibility for the persistence or accuracy of URLs for external or third-party Internet Websites referred to in this publication and does not guarantee that any content on such Websites is, or will remain, accurate or appropriate.

Designations used by companies to distinguish their products are often claimed as trademarks. All brand names and product names used in this book and on its cover are trade names, service marks, trademarks and registered trademarks of their respective owners. The publishers and the book are not associated with any product or vendor mentioned in this book. None of the companies referenced within the book have endorsed the book.

First edition

This book was professionally typeset on Reedsy.
Find out more at reedsy.com

I dedicate this book to my Husband who is my best friend and always by my side calling me to be the best version of myself. I couldn't do any of this without you.

Contents

One

Introduction

"There's no way to be a perfect mother and a million ways to be a good one."
-Jill Churchill

Hello, Mama! I am happy that you are here to read this little book on ways to find peace daily from the inherent anxiety that comes along with parenthood. I understand that many of us have had a great deal of anxiety before motherhood, as well. Welcome to the tribe! Being a mother is akin to being a superhero for our kids even though most days we do not feel this way. To our children, we are everything. The little things that we do daily matter. I am a believer in small steps in the right direction, small steps in a healing direction, and small steps in a loving direction toward ourselves and our beautiful children. You are taking that small step now by educating yourself and seeking solutions. Right now, give yourself a mental "thank you" and pat yourself on the back. You are doing a great job at being a parent and it shows!

First, let's discuss the symptoms of anxiety and how that can manifest for us mamas. Cerebral describes anxiety as a pattern of thinking about different ideas and events that are most often what they refer to as a cycle of disruptive thoughts. When we experience anxiety, we are may experience cycling thoughts, worry, difficulty managing thoughts, physical discomfort including chest pain, muscle soreness or aches, stomach pain, feeling lightheaded or dizzy, shortness of breath, avoidance of people, or circumstances, etcetera. The scale and intensity with which we experience these symptoms will differ from woman to woman. We all have our own circumstances internally and externally that affect our life experiences day in and day out. I continue to say, we because I am the *Anxious Mama* also. Once again, you are not alone, so many of us suffer from these crippling symptoms. The difference is that we do not have to be ruled by these symptoms. I choose to believe that there are ways that we can lessen, or dare I say eliminate, these symptoms over time by taking consistent actions for the sake of our self-love, our health, our wellbeing, and our families.

According to the National Alliance on Mental Health, "You Are Not Alone". As of the year 2020, anxiety disorders in the US affected 48 million people per year. In addition, the impact of the COVID-19 pandemic heavily impacted this incidence, increasing the number of mental health concerns for many Americans across the spectrum. Add to the picture the concerns of mothers (and fathers) for their children and it goes without saying, we have been through a collective trauma as a nation that has increased symptoms of anxiety tenfold. Misha Gajewski, a Forbes Healthcare contributor stated, "Moms are not okay", siting the pandemic's impact on anxiety and depression in the perinatal and postnatal periods for one in seven U.S. women.

According to the study, the percentage of mothers experiencing anxiety in the U.S. tripled during the pandemic. The fear of becoming infected with COVID-19 and bringing it home to our children, coupled with the recommended isolation added to the anxiety, and even depression symptoms, that mothers acutely experience after giving birth. I deeply understand this as I had just given birth to my son in July of 2019 then shortly after, the pandemic was in full effect. I remember the anxiety, worry, and terror that ensued thinking about my newborn or family catching COVID-19. I am a happily married mama of 4 beautiful children, who are at this time, 8 years old and under.

I created this book as a safe space to explore ways that we can have small wins from day to day in our motherhood journey while dealing with anxiety. What follows are 50 ways to find your own version of peace in your daily, very busy life. I have made the suggestions bite-sized since I know that having time to read a super long, in-depth book may not be realistic for new or let's say, seasoned moms. I hope that you can take away multiple suggestions to use in conjunction with each other since we are aiming at improving our lifestyle, not just our behavior. I will be noting the ideas that you can involve your children in, as I have found this to be helpful in my own experience in my treatment process with anxiety. My heart goes out to ALL mamas and my deep desire is for some of these suggestions to ease the burdens that we face and bring a newfound joy and hope into your life. Let's jump in, mama!

Two

Who's Taking Care of Mama?

"Keep taking time for yourself until you're you again." – Lalah Delia

Our first set of suggestions will include ways that you can implement your self-care routine daily. Self-care is an important part of a mama's routine and your health will ultimately have an impact on your mothering journey.

Breathe - How fantastic is it that one of the most effective coping skills for dealing with anxiety and stress involves breathing? We do not have to buy anything fancy or be fancy at all for that matter (as I sit here in my t-shirt and comfy, stretch pants). Multiple studies have shown that breathing exercises are effective at reducing anxiety in participants and can help different levels of anxiety from mild to panic attack mode. This can involve simply stopping what you are doing, standing, or taking a seat, taking a full deep breath in through your nose to fill your stomach, pausing for a moment, and then releasing the breath through your mouth. Take a moment now to practice this simple exercise for 5 full

4

breath cycles. How are you feeling afterward? The great thing about this is that this is something you can involve your children in that will teach them a new coping skill. Children experience anxiety and stress, too. Especially if you, their mama experience it regularly.

Hydrate - Ask yourself how much water you are drinking daily? Water intake or lack thereof can affect the functioning of our brain and have an impact on our mood. Through our various daily activities, our bodies lose water, and we need to replenish the water for our bodies to function properly. The Mayo Clinic suggests that women drink 11.7 cups of water a day to be at an optimal level. If you find water to be mostly boring like I do, there are an abundance of ideas for making water more fun with fruit, herbs, and even veggies.

Hot Showers and baths – I don't know about you, but a hot shower can make a world of difference when I am feeling overwhelmed with anxiety and stress. Ask a partner or family member to take the wheel with your child, or children and lock the door in the bathroom. The feeling of the hot water and the sound of the water can offer a sensory escape, even if the event is short-lived.

Set a Routine - Many times anxiety can set in when unexpected events happen or there is no clear plan of execution for the many tasks ahead in a mama's day. Take some time to map out what an ideal day looks like for you. Make your plan realistic and be open to revisions if the plan that you originally created does not work out. There may need to be adjustments over time. Remember to integrate your self-care into the routine wherever you can. When we create a routine, there can be more of a sense of control over our day, and it is containing for children to have a re-occurring routine that they can count on daily. A daily routine has been my parenting fail-safe.

Incorporate Stress-Reducing Foods – The Cleveland Clinic brought many dietitians together to compile a list of foods that can reduce anxiety and stress over time by reducing cortisol levels in the body. The foods that were suggested were foods high in Vitamin B, high in Omega-3 fatty acids, magnesium, protein, and gut-healthy foods that are fermented and rich in probiotics. A more extensive list of exact foods can be found in the Resources section since I know many moms may have different preferences and food allergies.

Reduce Sugar and Caffeine – As an avid coffee lover, this one honestly hurts a little. Though there is no denying sugar and caffeine influence our nerves and while they serve a purpose, the negatives may out weight the positives when it comes to our physical and mental health. There have been findings that the bodily effects of sugar and caffeine can mimic the symptoms of anxiety, even panic attack symptoms.

Improve your Sleep Habits – It can be true that people that suffer from anxiety have trouble sleeping and adding a new baby or some toddlers to the mix and you are sure to have your sleep world turned upside down. If you are unable to guarantee a full 8 hours of sleep with a new baby or toddler, try consistently going to bed and waking up at the same time daily. Many of us mamas are told by our doctors and nurses to sleep when our babies sleep which is a great opportunity. Set your naps to begin and end before 3 pm so that your bedtime is not thrown off later in the evening.

Grounding Exercises – In my wellness journey, I recently learned about Grounding Techniques, which are practices developed by mental health professionals to treat anxiety and a whole host of other mental health issues and conditions. These Grounding techniques help to bring your focus away from distressing emotions and thoughts into the moment through sensory interventions and intentionally refocusing your mind when your anxiety is spinning out of control. Try the 5-4-3-2-1 Method to count backward from 5 using your senses. First, identify 5 things you are hearing, 4 things you can see, 3 things you can touch, 2 things you can smell, and 1 thing you can taste. This can be used in an unbearable moment of anxiety when you need a real break from the experience.

Exercise – Work exercise time into your routine for multiple days a week, starting at even 10 minutes of movement if the whole idea of exercise overwhelms you to even think about. Starting small and consistent can help you build up your endurance over time. It will help with anxiety by diverting your thoughts away from the negative thoughts and even increasing your self-esteem as you go. That's what it has done for me and if I can do it, ANYONE can! My children have been inspired by my exercise journey and will work out with me sometimes. A benefit of exercise is it helps us to model this healthy behavior to our children at an age when kids want to be on their computers as often as possible as they get older.

Get outside – Find a safe, lovely, comfortable place outside where you can get a little sun and bring the baby and kids. This place may be at your own home or apartment or at a park that you love to go to with your child. If possible, I suggest finding parks in your town or city that have fences or gates around them so that you can sit at a safe distance and let the kids play. This way the mama and child can have a release. Getting outside has been proven to reduce stress so it is a win-win.

Decrease the Noise! – I don't know about you, but I am overly sensitive to noise, more so now than I have ever been in my life. Albeit, I do have 4 vocally charged children, so you do the math. Noise is a trigger to my experience of anxiety. Do you relate? If so, I suggest implementing quiet times into your routine like a family reading time at night before winding down for bed. Another affordable tool to consider is noise-reducing earbuds. A cool company to check out is Loop Earplugs America. They allow you to choose the level of noise reduction you need and are stylish at the same time.

Three

Support! Support! Support!

"We're all in this together. It's okay, to be honest. It's okay to ask for help. It's okay to say you're stuck, or that you're haunted, or that you can't begin to let go. We can all relate to those things. Screw the stigma that says otherwise. Break the silence and break the cycle, for you are more than just your pain. You are not alone. And people need other people." – Jamie Tworkowski

We all know the saying, "It takes a village to raise a child" and no parent can deny the truth of that saying. You need support on so many levels as a mama. The following suggestions are geared toward supporting your own journey inwardly and socially.

Drop the Comparisons – You are uniquely and beautifully you, mama. Anxiety, imperfections, flaws, and all! Your story is your own. Your circumstances are your own. Your gifts, strengths, and even weaknesses are your own. You cannot compare a pine tree to bamboo since they are inherently different. Practice embracing your mama's journey with love since you are doing the very best you can. The key work is *Practice* in changing this toxic habit we women have.

Please, I NEED a break! – Motherhood will push us to the limits of ourselves in every way. It is a fact, but we are still humans, not robots. We need a break. I cannot tell you how many times I have become full of anxiety and negative thoughts and broke down crying with my newborn in my arms, tears dripping on that beautiful, fresh baby skin. Ask your partner, family member, or trusted friend for some time to sleep, get out of the house for a little while, take a hot shower or bath, or whatever you need. This is essential.

Running Errands by Yourself – No one really tells you how hard it will be transitioning into motherhood. How you will lose most, if not all of the "me time" that you previously had. Speak to your partner or trusted family member or friend about supporting you in finding time to do some of the errands that need to be done by yourself. You will get out of the house, get some fresh air, feel like an adult for a while (no baby talk or endless toddler/older child requests), and you can even treat yourself if you want to.

Educate Yourself – Today we have an endless amount of information and knowledge at our fingertips online, in books, in magazines, all over! Grab a piece of paper or a notebook. Observe yourself daily, how do you feel in the morning, the afternoon, and at night? How is your mood? Your thoughts? Record what symptoms you are feeling when you experience anxiety. Find information on anxiety for yourself, the symptoms, and the treatments.

Speak with your Medical Provider – Bring your self-assessment to your medical provider and discuss your symptoms. Ask them for recommendations and treatment options. Keep your personal health assessments and physicals up to date to rule out any other physical stressors. If you just had a baby and are going in for your follow-up visits, tell your provider honestly about the mental health symptoms you are experiencing. Postpartum anxiety does exist! According to Postpartum Support International, 1 in 7 women experience postpartum symptoms of anxiety, panic, and depression. You are not alone, and these conditions are treatable.

Get Professional Help – In the past, mothers reaching out for mental health support were stigmatized and negative labels were placed on them. This added another layer of stress to an already worrisome condition and the judgments that we place on ourselves alone. Now in the year 2022, we have made strides in normalizing mental health treatment for anxiety, depression, ADHD and so many more common conditions that mamas face. Now we do not even have to leave our homes to get mental health support and care, which is truly revolutionary. Research local and online options for the treatment of anxiety. You can personalize your treatment options by race, culture, gender, etcetera for what you are most comfortable with.

Find a therapist – Many women find it beneficial to talk about their experiences with a counselor. Taking that first step is uncomfortable but the benefits far outweigh the discomforts. In my experience, there is a feeling of empowerment as I develop new skills that help me manage my anxiety and increase my calm as I parent my babies.

Consider Natural Remedies or Supplements – In addition to your healthy food choices and hydration, consider natural remedies and supplements that reduce anxiety symptoms. Consult your local natural health food store or holistic professional for a consultation.

Consider Medication – Consult your medical provider and/or a psychiatrist as a part of your treatment plan to consider medication options that could improve your wellbeing over time by reducing symptoms of anxiety, in addition, to talk therapy and the implementation of coping skills. You get to decide what path will be best for your own treatment.

Cultivate Consistency – None of these changes happen overnight! Do not give up on yourself. You matter more than you realize. Stick with your plans and when you fall off, get back up and start again. Each day is a new chance. Give yourself grace.

Four

Inner Work

"*Know your own happiness. You want nothing but patience- or give it a more fascinating name, call it hope.*" *-Jane Austen, Sense and Sensibility*

This chapter centers on suggestions for introspection and inner work that will increase self-esteem and confidence as you go deeper to the roots of your anxiety to gain insight.

Give Yourself Some Credit – When we are struggling with mental health issues, like anxiety, there can be a tendency to beat ourselves up over it, thinking that we are a bad mom, or we can feel guilty that our babies don't have a "normal" parent. I've got news for you. There is no such thing as quote-unquote normal. Each day when you wake up and see yourself in the mirror, give yourself a compliment for waking up today to do the best you can.

Journaling – Go out and get yourself a fun journal, better yet order it online if you cannot get out of the house. Journaling has been proven to reduce anxiety when you use it to write down what you are worried about. Free write your thoughts and emotions, list what you are good at and areas that you would like to improve, and how you plan to do it. There are great journals that help you record your self-care journey and moods, and you can look back at your progress over time. I really like the Self Planner journal by Poketo.com. Please note that I am not an affiliate of Poketo.com; I just really like this journal.

Mindfulness – There has been research that shows that the practice of mindfulness, which centers on bringing your attention to the present moment, can reduce anxiety and stress. There are multiple ways to practice mindfulness. The grounding techniques mentioned earlier can be a form of mindfulness. Often anxiety can bring us into the future or the past and give us the feeling of being outside of our bodies. Mindfulness practices can bring us back into our bodies by focusing our attention on the present moment using our senses. Mindfulness can help decrease rumination which is a state of focus on the past, on things that we cannot change.

Affirmations – Using affirmative statements, or affirmations daily or weekly can replace your negative thoughts, worries, and anxiety-provoking thoughts with empowering statements that move you toward your desired state of wellbeing. You can even write your own personal affirmations or statements that you find empowering. The use of affirmations can serve to reprogram your inner thoughts over time. You will be forming a new habit of healthy, positive thought.

Find Your Inspiration – The Merriam Webster Dictionary defines inspiration as an inspiring agent or influence. Find what inspires you in writing, art, music, fashion, or another field tailored to you. Immerse yourself in that inspiration to give yourself a break from unwanted thoughts or emotions. Remember what makes you happy, what brings you joy, and what makes you unique.

Mood Music – Multiple studies have proven that music has a beneficial effect on reducing anxiety. Make a playlist of the songs that calm you, lift your spirit, and make you feel good. Choose music with a positive, hopeful message preferably. There are hundreds of calming playlists online that have been created to be calming, stress-reducing, healing and to sleep.

Read Daily – Reading daily has a number of benefits on its own but reading can be especially helpful with mental health. As mamas that suffer from anxiety, we need time to relax and de-compress. Reading can offer us that time. Find a time to read for 10 to 30 minutes in your schedule. Choose a non-fiction book that helps you learn new coping skills and increases your knowledge to re-frame your thoughts. Choose a fiction book with a protagonist that you relate to or a storyline that grabs your attention. Enjoy the quiet time in your imagination!

Spend less time on social media – Social media can be a way to connect with friends and family. It can also be a time-consuming, mindless activity of scrolling through posts full of random, sometimes triggering topics. Schedule a time to get on social media with a time limit of how long you will stay there. Take an inventory, how long do you typically stay on social media per day? Note your mood and how it makes you feel after? Note your thoughts? You have total permission to take a vacation from social media altogether. It can be a breath of fresh air. Participating in social media is a choice, you are not obligated to do it.

Learn to Let Go – Learning to let go and be flexible is key to releasing the burden that parental anxiety places on us. There are many things that we cannot control despite our best efforts. We may believe that we have the best possible plan for the situation or the perfect way of doing something. In our own mind, we could be right but then there comes our child with their own way of doing the task at hand. Their way may be different than ours. This does not make their way wrong and ours right. Loosening our grip on what we can control and not control can reduce a lot of anxiety in the mother and the child.

Practice the Creative Arts – Using the creative arts on a regular basis can help you to redirect anxious thoughts and feelings. The arts offer another avenue of therapeutic intervention. If you are inclined toward the creative arts or simply enjoy being creative, identify creative projects that you can utilize including art-making, painting, coloring, crafts, embroidery, knitting, dance, making music, writing, and the list goes on. Your children can be included in the creative process in a project with you if you choose. We love to dance at my house and are known to have family dance parties on the weekends. We laugh and all the stress of the week melts away!

Dream Again – As a mama, at a certain point in your motherhood journey, it can feel like you have lost touch with yourself, and all your time is for the baby and kids (because nearly all of it is). The truth is that our children grow so fast and there will come a time when they spread their wings and fly. Remember your dreams and what matters to you. Maybe there are areas you still want to develop in yourself personally or professionally. Explore those areas and think with possibility. The sky is the limit.

Five

Communication is Key

"The way we talk to our children becomes their inner voice." — *Peggy O'Mara*

Here I want to equip you with suggestions related to healthy communication. Communication is such an important facet of relationships and parenting.

Include your Partner or Trusted Person – Talk to your spouse or trusted person about what you are experiencing and what triggers your experiences of increased anxiety and stress when you are in a calm state of mind. Having this discussion can prevent them from taking any outbursts personally and create more intimacy. Talk with your partner about ways to prevent anxiety in situations through mutual support, offering breaks, empathy, and understanding.

Identify Triggers – Have your journal handy in a central place at home and take some time to observe yourself thoughtfully. What triggers your anxiety throughout the day? Are there particular times that you are more likely to be anxious than others? Are there particular situations or people that trigger anxious thoughts and feelings? Write them down and compile a list for self-awareness. This list will help you explain your symptoms and experience with your loved ones and children in an age-appropriate way.

Recognize limitations – After identifying what triggers you, take a mental assessment of areas in which you feel that you can push the boundaries of your comfort zone for growth purposes. Take note of areas that are overwhelming and too much, that you feel you cannot handle. Acknowledge and accept that you have limitations and that that is okay. Once again, you do not have to be a perfect parent. In these areas, you can ask for help or plan for alternative solutions that feel safe for you.

Set Boundaries – Once you know your triggers and your limitations, you can begin to set healthy boundaries for the sake of your mental health to improve your wellbeing. Healthy boundaries are unique to each person. You decide what protections need to be in place with people and situations to create a safe space for you to flourish. Boundaries can be psychological, emotional, and physical. You decide what needs to be implemented.

Allow for imperfections – Perfectionism often goes hand in hand with anxiety and as it turns out there is *freedom* in imperfection! As we observe our children, we see this as they play freely, dance when they hear a good beat, and sing like they are performing for an audience. Our kids are not afraid of mistakes because that is how they learn. As we age expectations increase. Expectations can even sometimes increase to unrealistic levels that even we cannot ourselves cannot attain. Yet these are the expectations we hold over ourselves daily. Give yourself some leeway. Give your kids some leeway. Author Stephen Guise says, "the premise of imperfectionism – and this is the key – is that having lower standards does not equate to getting worse results". Let that sink in. Practice putting down your expectations and allowing yourself to be surprised.

Allow for Bad days – It is a fact. There will be bad days. Even when you have taken new steps to overcome your anxiety and practiced your new coping skills. These days will come. Practice speaking kindly to yourself on those days with care and compassion. Take extra care of yourself and know that tomorrow will be better.

Talk to your kids about anxiety – As your children get bigger, they will notice the emotions of their mama and even feel concerned. They may see us struggle with an issue or situation and see us lose our cool. This can be an opportunity to discuss with our child what we were feeling at that moment and even what it is like to experience anxiety, sadness, frustration, and other emotions. Children can feel anxiety too in new situations like their first day at school. We can help normalize the discussion of emotions and how to deal with emotions with our children to help them to develop emotional intelligence. When I have done this with my kids, there have been times that they said the sweetest things to me afterward that lifted my heart right out of what I was feeling.

Learning to say, "I am Sorry" – When you experience anxiety do you ever get angry? If you answered, yes, I am with you 100%. I can think of several times I have become irate as I cook dinner with arguing siblings in the living room, a toddler pulling on my pants asking me for chocolate milk, the TV blaring, another child calling my name, Mom-mom-mom!!! As I try to not burn the food, angry thoughts race through my head and I begin to yell. Sometimes things are said that we do not mean in a fiery moment of overwhelm. I have learned to humble myself after calming down to say, "I am sorry". There may be times when you sit or kneel to your child's height and apologize. A sorry may be needed for your significant other or trusted person even. Apologies and honesty increase intimacy in relationships.

Learning how to say "No" – When we consider communication and mental health, assertiveness is a topic that ranks high in importance. Essentially, assertive communication offers practical skills for communicating yes or no to persons and circumstances. As mamas, we often feel like we have to say 'yes' to everything, even if we are moving away from our boundaries and pushing our limitations. The problem is this sets us up for overwhelm, possible outbursts or panic attacks, and even burnout. If even the thought of being assertive triggers your anxiety, explore what may be making you feel this way. Journal about it. Before entering a conversation in which you need to assert yourself for the sake of honoring your boundaries or wellness plan, pre-mediate the content of what you plan on saying. Keep it simple and to the point by staying on topic. Practice these skills over time. As you learn about being assertive and practice assertive communication, it will begin to come more naturally to you.

Create a Wellness Plan – Create a plan for yourself that expresses your goals and aspirations for your health and wellness journey. I like the plan by Wellness Works NW, which takes into consideration 9 areas of life: social wellness, emotional wellness, mental wellness, spiritual wellness, environmental wellness, occupational wellness, intellectual wellness, physical wellness, and financial wellness. You can use a journal or a sketchbook to explore your wellness plan. You can even use the creative arts to explore these areas. The idea is to create positive feelings, positive thoughts, and positive emotions. You deserve it, mama! And so do your babies.

Six

The Arms of the Community, a Collective Hug!

"When the world feels uncontrollable and even dangerous, a hug can work wonders." – Marika Lindholm, Ph.D.

This chapter gives you suggestions with ideas for how you can get dialed into your community locally or online. A sense of community gives us mamas a larger sense of the interconnected nature of life so that we can share that with our children.

Faith & Spirituality – The National Alliance on Mental Health has found that faith and spiritual interest can have a positive effect on those suffering from mental health issues. Pursuing this is a deeply personal choice that each mama must make for herself. Many mamas find a great sense of connection and community in their faith and spirituality.

Connect with your Significant Other – For those mamas that are married or that have a significant other, parenting can take a toll on these relationships as the focus shifts from them to the new baby. Navigating these waters is especially important as your spouse can be a key supporter for you and the babies. Whenever possible, make time to share intimate moments with your spouse. The key is making time with your spouse a priority, not an afterthought.

Connect with supportive Family Members – If you have family around you, reach out to them. Family support can lift the burden of parenting by offering help with cooking, cleaning, babysitting, errands, and even planned dates with your spouse or friends. I understand that not every mama has family nearby and my heart goes out to you. Choose safe and supportive family members that understand your mental health concerns and support your personal well-being and your family's wellbeing.

Connect with Friends – Social support can work wonders for new and seasoned mamas alike! Do not go forward alone. Call on friends to hang out, schedule a phone call to chat and catch up, schedule a trip to a café or a walk at the park.

Find an online Group of like-minded Mamas – Social media platforms like Facebook and Twitter can offer a whole host of options for finding interactive groups of mamas to take part in. Connecting with other moms further hammers the idea that we are not the only ones experiencing challenges and difficulties in parenting. If you do not find one that you feel is a fit, you can create your own. You can also search locally if you are in a new place and want to meet some local mamas that you can meet up with and maybe even have play dates with the kids.

Just for fun, I suggest researching pages on Instagram dedicated to Mom memes. You will have some much-needed, loud, belly laughs when you see the hilarious memes other parents have created about this wacky, wild journey of parenthood! Side note: Laugh therapy is a thing.

Find an online Group in your area of interest – This is like finding the group for mamas but in your area of interest instead. The point is to find like-minded individuals to share ideas, inspiration, and knowledge.

Find a Professional Group that Supports your Career Goals – From my experience and many other mamas' experiences, career and finances can be an area of anxiety. Maybe you have a solid career, and your company is empathetic toward mothers, or maybe your journey into motherhood caused a major bump in your career plan. You had it all planned out, then there came a baby with his or her own agenda, and you are now back at square one! Whatever your situation professionally, there are many resources out there to support you in your profession, your career, or your new entrepreneurial endeavor. You can find groups that are in your professional area and gain new skills, hone skills you already have, and once again, be inspired and encouraged!

Find an Accountability Partner on Messenger – If being in a bigger group is not your style, search for an accountability partner who you can personal message online, speak with on the phone, and/or meet up to stay accountable for your treatment plan, your wellness plan, your mama goals, and your career goals.

Seven

Conclusion

"No language can express the power and beauty and heroism of a mother's love." – Edwin Chapman

As we have reached the end of this journey together, I want to give you a proverbial hug, mama. It has been a pleasure sharing these ideas with you. I believe in you. You have all the tools you need within you to have a wonderful life with your family. As you embark on this courageous journey of facing your anxiety, fear, and stress, things will get better. You will gain wisdom. You will flourish and blossom into the unique woman that you are. Your children will marvel at your beauty and tell of your lovely fragrance. Keep your head up and remember every day is a new beginning, a chance to start again... .no matter how many times it takes!

If you have found this book helpful, please leave a favorable review on Amazon and share this book with other mamas you think it would benefit. Thank You!

If ever you or a loved one need help with emotional distress, here are some resources for immediate help:

National Suicide Prevention Hotline: 1-800-273-8255

Crisis Text Line: Text Home to 741-741

Eight

References & Resources (in the order of Chapters)

Ramirez, P. (2020, October 2). *The Best Mom Quotes All Mothers Will Relate To*. The Habitat. Retrieved April 27, 2022, from https://thehabitat.com/life/the-best-mom-quotes-all-mothers-will-relate-to/10/

NAMI: National Alliance on Mental Illness. (2022, February 1). *Mental Health by the Numbers*. Retrieved April 28, 2022, from https://www.nami.org/mhstats

Gajewski, M. (2020, June 19). *Moms Are Not Okay: Pandemic Triples Anxiety And Depression Symptoms In New Mothers*. Forbes.Com. Retrieved April 28, 2022, from https://www.forbes.com/sites/mishagajewski/2020/06/19/moms-are-not-okay-coronavirus-pandemic-triples-anxiety-and-depression-in-new-mothers/?sh=642df60748ce

Cerebral. (n.d.). *Anxiety Treatment*. Cerebral.Com. Retrieved April 28, 2022, from https://cerebral.com/anxiety-treatment

Santos, J. (n.d.). *25 Self Care Quotes for Moms and Women*. But First, Joy. Retrieved April 28, 2022, from https://butfirstjoy.com/25-self-care-quotes-for-moms/?msclkid=99969871c67911ecab6b9abd6c1718d3

Ankrom, S. (2022, February 14). *Deep Breathing Exercises to Reduce Anxiety*. Verywell Mind. Retrieved April 28, 2022, from https://www.verywellmind.com/abdominal-breathing-2584115

Cambridge University Press. (2014, January 30). *Effects of hydration status on cognitive performance and mood*. Retrieved April 28, 2022, from https://www.cambridge.org/core/journals/british-journal-of-nutrition/article/effects-of-hydration-status-on-cognitive-performance-and-mood/1210B6BE585E03C71A299C52B51B22F7?msclkid=591a71cfc59211ec9384da9885507d44

Mayo Clinic Staff. (2020, October 14). *Water: How much should you drink every day?* Mayo Clinic. Retrieved April 28, 2022, from https://www.mayoclinic.org/healthy-lifestyle/nutrition-and-healthy-eating/in-depth/water/art-20044256?msclkid=31524d6fc59311ecbaa10b745344fdf3

Cleveland Clinic. (2021, June 15). *Eat These Foods to Reduce Stress and Anxiety*. Retrieved April 28, 2022, from https://health.clevelandclinic.org/eat-these-foods-to-reduce-stress-and-anxiety/?msclkid=b25d98b6c59511ec858f49de4b5ab4e0

Abraham, M. (2020, October 10). *Sugar and Anxiety: The Relationship*. CalmClinic. Retrieved April 28, 2022, from https://www.calmclinic.c

om/anxiety/causes/sugar?msclkid=59646fa1c59811ec9976573cd5a2
2adc

Harvard Health Publishing. (2020, October 13). *Tips for beating anxiety to get a better night's sleep.* Retrieved April 28, 2022, from https://www. health.harvard.edu/mind-and-mood/tips-for-beating-anxiety-to-get-a-better-nights-sleep?msclkid=f72bdc5fc59b11ecb18ec5b2d6166979

Raypole, C. (2019, May 24). *30 Grounding Techniques to Quiet Distressing Thoughts.* Healthline. Retrieved April 28, 2022, from https://www.heal thline.com/health/grounding-techniques?msclkid=ca26c878c5a011e c9b59438effe73a49

Ratey, J. J., MD. (2019, October 24). *Can exercise help treat anxiety?* Harvard Health Publishing. Retrieved April 28, 2022, from https://ww w.health.harvard.edu/blog/can-exercise-help-treat-anxiety-2019102 418096?msclkid=1d5d3959c5a311ecb33217ea0adeeb9b

Lindholm, M., Ph. D. (2017, February 7). *10 Anxiety Busters for Moms.* Psychology Today. Retrieved April 28, 2022, from https://www.psych ologytoday.com/us/blog/more-women-s-work/201702/10-anxiety-busters-moms

Your life, your volume | Loop Earplugs America – Loop United States

Staff, D. (2021, May 7). *71 Quotes to Remind You That You're Not Alone.* Delaware Psychological Services & Associates LLC. Retrieved April 28, 2022, from https://www.delawarepsychologicalservices.com/post/71 -quotes-to-remind-you-that-you-re-not-alone?msclkid=7dbe2913c6 7a11ecbaa2f8c495a88ee5

Radniecki, L. (2021, October 12). *Anxiety in motherhood: How I learned to calm and control my fears.* Motherly. Retrieved April 28, 2022, from https://www.mother.ly/life/anxiety-in-motherhood-how-i-learned-to-calm-and-control-my-fears/

Hine, R. H., Maybery, D. J., & Goodyear, M. J. (2019, March 8). *Identity in Personal Recovery for Mothers With a Mental Illness.* National Library of Medicine. Retrieved April 28, 2022, from https://www.ncbi.nlm.nih.gov/pmc/articles/PMC6418025/?msclkid=47d3c472c63911eca97 61a02382f8709

Postpartum Support International - PSI

NAMI: National Alliance on Mental Illness. (n.d.). *Finding a Mental Health Professional.* Retrieved April 28, 2022, from https://www.nami.org/Your-Journey/Individuals-with-Mental-Illness/Finding-a-Mental-Health-Professional

Office of Communications. (2019, August 12). *Moms' Mental Health Matters: Depression and Anxiety Around Pregnancy.* NIH: Eunice Kennedy Shriver National Institute of Child Health and Human Development. Retrieved April 28, 2022, from https://www.nichd.nih.gov/ncmhep/initiatives/moms-mental-health-matters/moms

Goodreads. (n.d.). *Self Actualization Quotes (191 quotes).* Goodreads.Com. Retrieved April 28, 2022, from https://www.goodreads.com/quotes/tag/self-actualization?msclkid=022a3060c67c11ecb626034d27f1cbce

Scott, E., PhD. (2021, April 1). *How to Journal When You Have Anxiety.* Verywell Mind. Retrieved April 28, 2022, from https://www.verywellmind.com/journaling-a-great-tool-for-coping-with-anxiety-314467

2

Self Planner – Poketo

Kind, S., B. A., & Hofmann, S. G., PhD. (2016, February 10). *Facts about the effects of mindfulness*. Anxiety.Org. Retrieved April 28, 2022, from https://www.anxiety.org/can-mindfulness-help-reduce-anxiety?msc lkid=2ad153fdc67511ecb0dddff93d8aa4df

Inspiration. (n.d.). The Merriam-Webster.Com/Dictionary. Retrieved April 28, 2022, from https://www.merriam-webster.com/dictionary/ inspiration?msclkid=b979599bc67711eca8981845dbc0564c

Gordon, A. (2019, January 28). *7 Ways Reading Can Help Your Mental Health*. AwakenTheGreatnessWithin.Com. Retrieved April 28, 2022, from https://www.awakenthegreatnesswithin.com/7-ways-reading-can-help-your-mental-health/

McDowell, D. (2018, November 27). *7 Ways Taking a Break from Social Media Can Help You Reduce Stress and Anxiety*. New Beginnings Therapy. Retrieved April 28, 2022, from http://newbeginningstherapy.com/taki ng-a-break-from-social-media-reduce-stress-and-anxiety/?msclkid= 5eca2e36c69a11ecae9ab30dd8131ba2

W. (2021, June 20). *Motherhood anxiety: 10 practical tips to control mom anxiety*. Messy Yet Lovely. Retrieved April 28, 2022, from https://mess yyetlovely.com/deal-with-motherhood-anxiety/

Rosen, M. P. (2014, September 22). *Reduce anxiety with creative arts therapies*. Anxiety.Org. Retrieved April 28, 2022, from https://www.a nxiety.org/creative-arts-offer-innovative-approaches-to-traditional-therapy?msclkid=7db0317fc69d11eca2b0a50599456c9c

Everyday Power. (n.d.). *Communication Quotes and Sayings to Strengthen Relationships*. Retrieved April 28, 2022, from https://everydaypower .com/communication-quotes-and-sayings/#:%7E:text=Communicati on%20quotes%20and%20sayings%20to%20strengthen%20relationshi ps.%201,work%20at%20it.%E2%80%9D.%20%E2%80%93%20John%2 0Powell.%20More%20items?msclkid=59713339c6a111ec9e24dd8bb 117ea27

Winters, V. (2019, February 6). *Being a Parent When You Have Anxiety*. NAMI: National Alliance on Mental Illness. Retrieved April 28, 2022, from https://www.nami.org/Blogs/NAMI-Blog/February-2019/Bei ng-a-Parent-When-You-Have-Anxiety

Katz, B. (2022, February 3). *How to Avoid Passing Anxiety on to Your Kids*. Child Mind Institute. Retrieved April 28, 2022, from https://chil dmind.org/article/how-to-avoid-passing-anxiety-on-to-your-kids/# explain-your-anxiety

Caridad, K. (2020, December 7). *BEING A PARENT WITH SOCIAL ANXIETY*. National Social Anxiety Center. Retrieved April 28, 2022, from https://nationalsocialanxietycenter.com/2020/05/30/being-a-p arent-with-social-anxiety/

Selva, J., Bc. S. Psychologist. (2022, March 28). *How to Set Healthy Boundaries: 10 Examples + PDF Worksheets*. PositivePsychology.Com. Retrieved April 28, 2022, from https://positivepsychology.com/great-self-care-setting-healthy-boundaries/

Guise, S. (2015). *How to Be an Imperfectionist: The New Way to Self-*

Acceptance, Fearless Living, and Freedom from Perfectionism (1st ed.). Selective Entertainment LLC.

Ethington, M. (2020, November 17). *When Your Anxiety Makes You An Angry Mom*. Scary Mommy. Retrieved April 28, 2022, from https://ww w.scarymommy.com/moms-anxiety-makes-her-angry

Funny Mom Meme site on Instagram: https://www.instagram.com/ sarcastic_mommy/

Peterson, T. J., MS, NCC, DAIS. (2014, September 18). *Anxiety and Assertiveness: Four Tips | HealthyPlace*. Healthy Place. Retrieved April 28, 2022, from https://www.healthyplace.com/blogs/anxiety-schman xiety/2014/09/anxiety-and-assertiveness-four-tips?msclkid=1b94d8 b4c70011ec81c98b90aef8df4e

Clemenson, S. D. (2020, September 8). *What is a Wellness Plan?* Wellness Works NW. Retrieved April 28, 2022, from https://www.wellnesswor ksnw.com/what-is-a-wellness-plan/?msclkid=e63471fec70511ec8fe 8367ef9f795cb

NAMI: National Alliance on Mental Illness. (n.d.-a). *Faith & Spirituality*. Retrieved April 28, 2022, from https://www.nami.org/Your-Journey/ Individuals-with-Mental-Illness/Faith-Spirituality

Creative Healthy Family. (2022, January 14). *31 Inspirational Motherhood Quotes About Being a Good Mom*. Retrieved April 28, 2022, from https://www.creativehealthyfamily.com/inspirational-motherhood-quotes/?msclkid=c1623bb4c71411ecadaf9f50a3d214e6

About the Author

Brittany Kay Baez is a Master's level Creative Arts Counselor, originally from Denver, Colorado, now living in beautiful North Carolina. She is passionate about all things family and has 4 beautiful children with her amazing husband. Brittany has a vision for improved mental health for families and the youth.

Made in the USA
Thornton, CO
06/20/22 21:59:05

3e758c57-6ef8-4a08-846a-e689f279467eR01